T0209308

ANOTHER BOOK

Jesus in John's Apocalypse

Jonathon Cutchins

WESTBOW
PRESS®
A DIVISION OF THOMAS NELSON
& ZONDERVAN

WestBow Press books may be ordered through booksellers or by contacting:

WestBow Press
A Division of Thomas Nelson & Zondervan
1663 Liberty Drive
Bloomington, IN 47403
www.westbowpress.com
844-714-3454

All Scripture quotations are taken from the New King James Version. Copyright © 1982 by Thomas Nelson, Inc. Used by permission. All rights reserved.

ISBN: 979-8-3850-0391-4 (sc)
ISBN: 979-8-3850-0392-1 (hc)
ISBN: 979-8-3850-0393-8 (e)

Library of Congress Control Number: 2023913649

Print information available on the last page.

WestBow Press rev. date: 10/30/2023

Dedication

This book is dedicated (in chronological order) to Katie, Taylor, Jack, Eliyana, Kingsley, Lily, Laney, Susannah, Josiah, and to all the other children I have called my own. It was preached and is written in one simple hope—that you might have comfort in the coming trouble, might not be in terror of the Lord's judgment and return, but might say with sincere feeling, "Come quickly, Lord Jesus."

Acknowledgements

First, I would like to thank the Lord Jesus Christ, who separated me to His Gospel, calls me daily from my own imagined wisdom into His glorious foolishness, and whose judgments I don't understand but fill me with hope and trust. Second, I would like to thank my wife for her patience (yes, you, for your patience), for keeping a small army of kids out of my hair while I devote hours I don't have to my second nonpaying job, for encouraging me in what must seem like a very improbable task and one not calculated to accomplish anything. Third, I would like to thank my children whose smiles and love make all my failures seem irrelevant. Fourth, I would like to thank the church that meets in the Henson Poolhouse, formerly known as Christ Reformed Church. Without the encouragement and inspiration given me by you all, none of this would have happened.

Contents

CHAPTER ONE
The Conqueror

The White Horse and his Rider

Originally preached August 4, 2019

"WE ARE WRONG ABOUT EVERYTHING ELSE, BUT we are right about the Gospel." It's a pretty good one-liner, and I have been using it as the unofficial motto of our church. "We are wrong about everything else, but we are right about the Gospel." What I mean to imply is that the Gospel is the only thing that matters. The Gospel, quite literally, justifies all our other mistakes, errors, and failures. So, I don't know how far our little look into the book of Revelation will get, but the key that I intend to use is something like this: "I am wrong about eschatology. I am wrong about numerology. I am wrong about symbolism. But I intend to be right about what the Revelation says about Christ." Where it is necessary to try to interpret John's visions to tell my story, I don't intend to seek a coherent system of symbolism, and I don't intend to offer any opinion on the chronology of the "end-times," not even in the most general of ways. Instead, I will shamelessly use all the imagery and mysticism to try to illustrate the Christ of Revelation. I learned many years ago that Christ does not share His secrets to gratify our curiosity or make us knowledgeable or inflate our egos. There are things that can only be understood by taking them in your hand and seeking the Gospel in them for the purpose of comforting the Lord's people. I think that, if we will

take the dark and mysterious things in scripture and preach the Gospel from them, we will find that the mystery clears up rather more easily than we expected.

> And I saw in the right hand of Him who sat on the throne a scroll written inside and on the back, sealed with seven seals. Then I saw a strong angel proclaiming with a loud voice, "Who is worthy to open the scroll and to loose its seals?" And no one in heaven or on the earth or under the earth was able to open the scroll, or to look at it. So I wept much, because no one was found worthy to open and read the scroll, or to look at it. (Revelation 5:1–4)

I've been told quite often that I have an overabundance of confidence. People ask me regularly why I am so cocky. So let me start right off by telling you that I can't open this scroll and can't explain the Revelation for myself or for you. This scroll, I am relatively confident, is what chapter 1, verse 1, calls "the Revelation of Jesus Christ, which God gave Him to show His servants," and I hope to tell you the story of God giving Christ that revelation—a revelation not of the end of the world, not of the Antichrist, not of judgment and condemnation but of the one who was dead and lives forevermore and has made us kings and priests to His God and Father, and holds the keys to death and hell.

So, our story starts in the throne room of Heaven, and like all good stories, we run into a problem fairly quickly. God has a scroll with stuff written all over it; it is jam-packed with goodness, full of grace and truth. This scroll is, as I suggested earlier, the Revelation itself—not just the weird book at the end of our Bible but the "express image of God." This is everything you need to know about who God is, which in the long run is everything you need to know about everything. Our Lord said. "this is eternal life, that they may know You, the only true God, and Jesus Christ whom You have sent." (John 17:3) This story is about the Lord and His salvation. Everything else is just the stage on which that action takes place. Let's not get so distracted by the scenery that we miss the story, the knowledge of God contained in the scroll. But, as we already knew, that knowledge isn't easy to come by.

Let's back up a little to chapter 4 of Revelation to set the scene.

> Immediately I was in the Spirit; and behold, a throne set in heaven, and One sat on the throne. And He who sat there was like a jasper and a sardius stone in appearance; and there was a rainbow around the throne, in appearance like an emerald. Around the throne were twenty-four thrones, and on the thrones I saw twenty-four elders sitting, clothed in white robes; and they had crowns of gold on their heads. And from the throne proceeded lightnings, thunderings, and

voices. Seven lamps of fire were burning before the throne, which are the seven Spirits of God.

Before the throne there was a sea of glass, like crystal. And in the midst of the throne, and around the throne, were four living creatures full of eyes in front and in back. The first living creature was like a lion, the second living creature like a calf, the third living creature had a face like a man, and the fourth living creature was like a flying eagle. The four living creatures, each having six wings, were full of eyes around and within. And they do not rest day or night, saying:

"Holy, holy, holy, Lord God Almighty, Who was and is and is to come!"

Whenever the living creatures give glory and honor and thanks to Him who sits on the throne, who lives forever and ever, the twenty-four elders fall down before Him who sits on the throne and worship Him who lives forever and ever, and cast their crowns before the throne, saying:

"You are worthy, O Lord, To receive glory and honor and power; For You created all things, And by Your will they exist and were created." (Revelation 4:2–11)

So this is a pretty neat crew. In our story, however, the significance of all these people is that they can't help us read the scroll. We have got twenty-four of the sharpest cats around. They can stand for the sum of human knowledge if we want to get symbolic. They have got it together. But they are no help at all to poor old John; they can't even open or read the scroll for themselves, so they are certainly no help to him or us. We have four weirdo angel things. They've got bunches of wings and bunches of eyes, and they kind of represent all the living things in Creation. You have got the king of the jungle, the lion; the king, or at least representative, of domesticated animals, the cow; the king of birds; and man himself.[1] But the bottom line is that they are no help. Nobody "in heaven or on the earth or under the earth" (Revelation 5:3) could give us the only news that is unconditionally good. One last character we need to look at in this light before we move on is the guy on the throne.

God created the worlds by His Word. The ultimate purpose of Creation is that there would be people who are not Him (that's us), who are like Him, are sons and daughters to Him, and are kings and priests to Him. It is the knowledge of Him, the scroll, that makes us like Him. But even omnipotence must have a

---

[1] When the scroll is finally opened, they each seem to have some kind of connection to what is written under one particular seal, so they are some sort of messengers of the Gospel, but I won't be dealing with their specifics in this book.

Way. And the Way to Him is not to approach God enthroned in Heaven. The old myths all say that to see God in His glory is to be undone; for us to see Him, He has to take human form. Well, they aren't wrong, but what the mythmakers and philosophers and priests of all stripes have never realized is that it isn't merely seeing God in His glory with our eyes but viewing Him in our thoughts and feelings is futile and self-destructive too. The Way to God, whether physically, mentally, spiritually, emotionally, or in any way whatsoever, to give away the punchline, which I assume most of you have seen coming, is through the man Jesus Christ, our Immanuel.

> So I wept much, because no one was found worthy to open and read the scroll, or to look at it. But one of the elders said to me, "Do not weep. Behold, the Lion of the tribe of Judah, the Root of David, has prevailed to open the scroll and to loose its seven seals."
>
> And I looked, and behold, in the midst of the throne and of the four living creatures, and in the midst of the elders, stood a Lamb as though it had been slain, having seven horns and seven eyes, which are the seven Spirits of God sent out into all the earth. Then He came and took the scroll out of the right hand of Him who sat on the throne. (Revelation 5:4–7)

Now, I emphatically think we must go to the man Himself—the walking, talking, weeping, partying Christ of the Gospels—to learn who God is. The essence of God, that which makes Him who He is, is not found in what the theologians term the "attributes of God": omnipotence, omniscience, eternity, immutability, and that whole raft of overeducated nonsense. Instead, His essence is found in the divine-human compassion when He sees us as sheep without a shepherd. It is found in the weeping for the death of His friend. It is found in the rage at the corruption of His Father's house by the "moneymen." But the big theme of the book of Revelation, which even the worst commentators have picked up on, the big theme of the Bible, and the big theme of the scroll is death. When John tells us this story, very tellingly, it is not the loving Christ or the bereaved Christ or the angry Christ who reveals God to us. It is the dead Christ; he presents us with a lamb slain. It is the dead Christ who draws all men unto Himself. It is the slain Christ who sends the Spirits of God into all the earth with the good news. It is the slain Christ who tore the veil of the temple, uniting God and man, which is exactly what the scroll we are finally going to get a look at is about.

I don't mean to gloss over the rest of chapter 5, but for our story, it can be summed up as "And all the autobots said, 'Yay, Optimus!'" So let's get to what the scroll actually says.

> Now I saw when the Lamb opened one of the seals;
> and I heard one of the four living creatures saying
> with a voice like thunder, "Come and see." And I

> looked, and behold, a white horse. He who sat on it
> had a bow; and a crown was given to him, and he
> went out conquering and to conquer. (Revelation
> 6:1–2)

If, as I have posited, this is about revealing Christ to us, what exactly are we supposed to see here? Our translation says "one of the four living creatures." It should probably be read more like "the first of the living creatures," living creature number one, the lion. The One on the horse has a bow, an offensive weapon, a crown signifying victory, and He is presented as winning whatever fight it is He is in. But conquest is about more than victory, He doesn't just beat His opponent, He takes what was the opponent's and makes it His.

Human history is the story of putting God in a box. In Eden, Adam and Eve knew that the vast majority of their good came from God, but they thought that there was something good that came from another source, their own choice, their own knowledge, their own will, a fruit, a snake, something. We have progressively looked for more of our good from other sources and less from God; we have made the box that we put God in smaller and smaller. Most of the things in our lives that we hope for, that we think will be good, we are looking for from sources other than God. Of course, eventually we got God, literally, in a little golden box—the famous Ark of the Covenant, a box that is really good at a few things, in a few places, on very select occasions. The God

in the box is the greatest picture of the Law that I know.[2] And any type of religion that puts God in a box—any box—is legalism. Contrast the God in the box with Satan roaming the Earth as a lion, hunting, stalking his prey. And so, the first thing we need to know about Christ and His Gospel is that He isn't staying in the

---

[2] Throughout I use the term *Law* following Martin Luther, as best exampled in his commentary on Galatians, which I recommend to better understand this usage and point of view. Law refers to the idea that God's involvement in our lives is based on our actions and motives, as opposed to the Gospel which teaches that God involves Himself with us as if the actions and motives of Christ are our own. Law then is a way of understanding the world, a powerful psychological cause and effect of sin. In Paul's writings Law specifies a form of righteousness (as well as the unrighteousness of nonconformance), distinct from and antagonistic to the form of righteousness which is given to us by the Gospel namely imputation of the life and works of Christ. While legal righteousness would be obvious if encountered, Gospel righteousness is largely imperceptible to us and when perceived does not seem to be righteous as it is inconceivable to the mind of Edenic, fallen, and redeemed man (perhaps even inconceivable to us in the life to come).

Although Gospel righteousness is produced by a verdict of the divine court, it should not be considered merely *forensic*. Verdicts of a human court are an acknowledgement of preexisting truth. However, in the divine verdict of justification we are not recognized as righteous. Rather the creative Word calls our righteousness into being. The pronouncement is not so much akin to, "I find you not guilty." as "I now pronounce you man and wife." Thus, the whole of the Law—performance on the one hand and failure on the other both with their attendant consequences—is entirely finished, such that nothing more should be expected from that quarter. Distinguishing between Law and Gospel is helpful to the renewing of the mind. (Hat tip to Taylor Henson and P.J. Arms)

box anymore, and when He came riding out, He tore the veil that separates God and man. Is the lion a symbol of kingly royalty? Sure, I guess so. But here I think what we especially need to see is God out of the box, going out "conquering and to conquer," roaming the earth, going to and fro, a predator hunting as we are told Satan does.

In our minds, evil has a few advantages. Christ has humbled Himself to take those advantages as His own. I don't want to pretend to have any great keys to John's Apocalypse but this theme of Christ doing things that we usually associate with Satan—that Christ has gone not merely into the lowest class of society but into the criminal class, literally hanging with thieves—may be one reason we have found this book of the first who are last and the last who are first so confusing. Anyway, onward.

He carries a bow. Of course, the most famous bow that God carried is the one that He hung in the clouds. And I think that maybe it is with good reason that the book of Revelation is literally drenched in rainbows. He hung up the bow of judgment because He swore never again to flood the Earth with condemnation. That is the bow that we should see in His hand, taken up to flood the Earth, this time with grace and mercy. The weapon of God's wrath has been remade; Our Lord reforged the bow in the fires of Hell when He descended there, and now it has become a bow of mercy so that we may not only say with the prophets that His arm is not shortened (Isaiah 59:1), but we may go further and say that the God of the Gospel is mightier than ever the God of Law could hope to be. In the Gospel, death and condemnation have themselves become the waters of baptism, have become life and justification.

Before I ever read any theology or was a serious student of the scripture at all, when I was just a boy sitting in an English lit class, I read a poem. And years later, when I found all the things I had put my trust in—mainly myself—to be empty hopes, the poem came back to me and gave me a different hope. Here is John Donne's Holy Sonnet XIV

> Batter my heart, three-person'd God, for you
>
> As yet but knock, breathe, shine, and seek to mend;
>
> That I may rise and stand, o'erthrow me, and bend
>
> Your force to break, blow, burn, and make me new.
>
> I, like an usurp'd [captured by an enemy] town to another due,
>
> Labor to admit you, but oh, to no end;
>
> Reason, your viceroy in me, me should defend,
>
> But is captiv'd, and proves weak or untrue.
>
> Yet dearly I love you, and would be lov'd fain,
>
> But am betroth'd [promised, engaged to be married] unto your enemy;

Divorce me [from Satan], untie or break that knot again,

Take me to you, imprison me, for I,

Except you enthrall [enslave] me, never shall be free,

Nor ever chaste, except you ravish [rape] me.

No one can take what belongs to the strong man unless he is first bound. I don't feel like looking up the text; we all know Christ said that. Well, the strong man is Satan, and as Donne puts it so eloquently, we are "betrothed" to the enemy of Christ; that is, we are bound to sin and death by the Law which is holy and just and good. All my hope had left me that I would ever be a Christian. So many preachers have stood up and told us how easy it is to become a Christian, but I never found it that way. If Christ was knocking on the door of my heart, part of me would run to open the door, but another part always slammed it in His face. It happened over and over again, and I finally realized that the real me, the truest strongest part of me, was the part that rejected Christ.

And in that hopelessness, I thought a new thought. I had never heard of Irresistible Grace. I thought Calvin was some nutjob, and Calvinism a one-trick predestination pony. I never imagined that the rider of the white horse, the Prince who saves the day for me, the truly good news was there.

What if Christ knocks on the door of your heart, and you don't open it? What then? Is that the end of the story, or is my hope—like Dr. Donne's hope, that Christ might batter down the door of our hearts that we refuse to open to Him true? All that is in me sides with Satan to my own destruction, but Christ stoops and humiliates Himself to conquer me. Those who criticize Irresistible Grace say that Christ is a Gentleman and will never force His affection on us. All I can say is that, if He doesn't, we will never have it or Him. To be a Saviour, He must be a conqueror, a heel, the bad guy.

We chose the serpent in the Garden. We choose him all the time, and the Law holds us to our choice, makes us keep our promises and pay our debts to darkness. We are the property, the promised bride of the strong man, destined to be his, but the weakness of God is a gracious Conqueror riding forth to our salvation, and neither Law, nor Satan, nor our own foolish will can prevent the Prince on the white horse from carrying off His princess.

I want to close with a question and one last picture. Where is the rider of the white horse riding His horse? I have talked a lot about King Saul lately, and his story, his descent into madness, darkness, and death, is emblematic of the God in the box and the Law. What has Christ really changed? Simply that, in the New Testament, there is another Saul whose story doesn't end in pointless war and madness. God got out of His box and went charging down the Damascus Road. The vision that I want to

close with is the vision that changed another Saul into Paul. That is the true conquest of the One who has gone out conquering and to conquer, the greatest of the legalists, the Pharisee of Pharisees become Grace's most uncompromising champion. Be ye converted.

CHAPTER 2
Left Behind? Just Don't Call Me Late for Dinner

The Black Horse

Originally Preached October 6, 2019

SOMETIME DURING MY CHILDHOOD, THE geniuses behind the American Christian experience came up with the idea of the Judgment House. A haunted house where God is the monster must have seemed like a great way to get people to trust God. The message is quite literally turn or burn, with the last scene being a courtroom where God throws away anybody who doesn't make the cut. The message is this: God can either be your best friend or your worst enemy.

But who wants to be friends with a guy who throws people away? And how can you ever trust someone who might waste you if you don't measure up? Maybe the reason this brand of Christianity targets kids so much is that they are still naive enough to think that they might measure up if the bar is low enough. The rest of us have realized by now that, no matter how easy the test, we will ultimately fail.

Of course, the Judgment Houses and their sequel, the Tribulation Trail, a drive-through tour of the end of the world, are jam packed with apocalyptic imagery. We all see the apocalypse as scenes of God smashing the sinners. I have been terrified by the book of Revelation for as long as I can remember. There's nothing special about that though is there? We are all terrified by this bizarre story that hangs over Christianity as an ominous specter of the future. It claims to be a revelation of Jesus Christ, but why is this Jesus so different from the Jesus of the Gospels? I want to take you on a ride through the apocalypse that is a little bit different. I believe that wrath and judgment are merely costumes, admittedly dark and strange, that grace wears when the situation calls for it, and I am going to try and survey Revelation for the purpose of pulling back the mask. Buckle up. It's gonna be wild!

Revelation is structured something like this: It begins with an introduction and some letters to various churches, which have some judgmental aspects, but I am going to dive straight into the entire end of the world sequence, which is so upsetting to us. We talked about the throne room of Heaven and the opening of the scroll last time, and that is kind of where the story kicks off. From an overview, the story begins with the first six seals on the scroll being opened. They trigger events that seem strange but don't so much frighten as they do confuse. Then there is a story about God's people being given a protective mark and a group too large to be numbered coming to Heaven and worshipping around the throne. Then the last seal is opened. Then there is a sequence of six trumpets being blown, each unleashing a rather plainer and rather "judgier" set of events than the seals did. This is where things start to get nasty with things falling out of the sky to smack the earth and monsters coming out of holes and whatnot. Then we have a series of stories about John and the

mighty angel with the little book, the two witnesses killed in the bad city, followed by the seventh trumpet and the saints in Heaven. Then we see the woman giving birth to a Child who ascends to the throne of God leading to the war in Heaven. Then the beasts who deceive the world are introduced followed by the reaping of the world's harvest. Then we get back to the judgment sequence with seven bowl judgments, which are the nastiest yet and several seem to be specifically designed to goad the beast and his followers into a fight with the Lamb. This is followed by the fall of Babylon. Then we have several stories from chapter 6 retold and expanded—Christ the Conqueror, Christ the Warrior, Christ the Judge, Christ with the keys of Death and Hell. Finally, we are shown the end.

So, we have a series of very strange, almost unintelligible stories about the kingdom and grace and judgment told in rather vague terms so as to give them a universal application. (Thanks to Father Robert Capon for much of the vision that wrote this chapter.) The stories are told with almost no names; instead, everyone has titles: the child, the woman, the dragon, the unjust steward, the lamb, the king's son, the saints, the witnesses, the older brother. You might have noticed that I mixed in several characters from the Parables of Jesus. I did that because that is how these stories strike me. The apocalypse is almost like "The Parables of Jesus Part II." And just for clarification, I think it is clear that these events, like those in Jesus's parables, are actual events although the timing and locations are unclear. Neither the parables nor the apocalypse is a fictional story, but both are told deliberately in a way that separates them from their local and historical context to give them universal application. It is in that light that I want to look at these stories.

I want to begin by proposing a framework to understand the structure of Revelation, especially the way it seems to tread the same ground several times.

> Now when one of those who sat at the table with Him heard these things, he said to Him, "Blessed is he who shall eat bread in the kingdom of God!"

> Then He said to him, "A certain man gave a great supper and invited many, and sent his servant at supper time to say to those who were invited, 'Come, for all things are now ready.' But they all with one accord began to make excuses. The first said to him, 'I have bought a piece of ground, and I must go and see it. I ask you to have me excused.' And another said, 'I have bought five yoke of oxen, and I am going to test them. I ask you to have me excused.' Still another said, 'I have married a wife, and therefore I cannot come.' So that servant came and reported these things to his master. Then the master of the house, being angry, said to his servant, 'Go out quickly into the streets and lanes of the city, and bring in here

the poor and the maimed and the lame and the blind.' And the servant said, 'Master, it is done as you commanded, and still there is room.' Then the master said to the servant, 'Go out into the highways and hedges, and compel them to come in, that my house may be filled. For I say to you that none of those men who were invited shall taste my supper.'" (Luke 14:15–24)

So, when we talk about judgment in Revelation, we are talking about the righteousness of the rider of the white horse when He judges, and we are also talking about this verse:

> When He opened the third seal, I heard the third living creature say, "Come and see." So I looked, and behold, a black horse, and he who sat on it had a pair of scales in his hand. And I heard a voice in the midst of the four living creatures saying, "A quart of wheat for a denarius, and three quarts of barley for a denarius; and do not harm the oil and the wine." (Revelation 6:5–6)

Now it is my opinion that these two sets of imagery depict the same Person, the colors of the horses notwithstanding.[3] And while the rider of the black horse is often described as famine,

---

[3] These sermons were preached in the order of Revelation 19 in which judgment comes before making war as opposed to the opposite order in Revelation 6.

I assume, because these prices are rather high, that assignment depends on a lot of assumptions which I am not concerned to support or attack, but I don't think that inference is helpful to understand the passage. Rather, what we should see is that the Lord rules the economy and the environment in which we live, and the circumstances of our lives are ordered to support our eternal selves. Simply put, "all things work together for good for those who are called according to His purpose" (Romans 8:28).

We see then that there are three sequences of judgments in Revelation: the seals, the trumpets, and the bowls. I think that we can understand them by comparing them to the three calls issued to the great banquet in Luke 14. The seals are the invitation to know God to those whom we expect to receive such a call—the Church people, the Christians, and the Jews. So, once Christ opened the scroll, whenever in history or the future we think that might be, the knowledge of God became available to anyone who cared to read the scroll. The scroll presented Christ as the conqueror, the judge, the warrior, and the one with power over death and hell. (The warrior and death and hell are dealt with in chapters 3 and 4.) But as the fifth seal tells us:

> When He opened the fifth seal, I saw under the altar the souls of those who had been slain for the word of God and for the testimony which they held. And they cried with a loud voice, saying, "How long, O Lord, holy and true, until You judge and avenge our blood on those who dwell on the

earth?" Then a white robe was given to each of them; and it was said to them that they should rest a little while longer, until both the number of their fellow servants and their brethren, who would be killed as they were, was completed. (Revelation 6:9–11)

The number of people who came to His party, who traded in their lives for His death was insufficient for the party He had planned. The group who was first invited to Christ's party—the religious, the Jews, us—are kept out of the place He has gone to prepare for us. We are not kept out by a judge who finds us lacking; rather, we are kept out by our own works, our own plans to build His kingdom and our kingdom, our own self-righteousness. The picture that we should have of the judgment is not of people beating on the doors of Heaven and Christ picking and choosing who can enter, but people determinedly, eagerly running into hell and the rider of the white horse vetoing our evil wills at His own discretion and with no cause but His Father's good pleasure, and dragging us to Heaven kicking and screaming (as I intend to demonstrate in chapter 5). And the sixth seal gives us the reason why we will not trust Him or His offer of mercy:

I looked when He opened the sixth seal, and behold, there was a great earthquake; and the sun became black as sackcloth of hair, and the moon became like blood. And the stars of heaven fell to the earth, as a fig tree drops its late figs when it is

shaken by a mighty wind. Then the sky receded as a scroll when it is rolled up, and every mountain and island was moved out of its place. And the kings of the earth, the great men, the rich men, the commanders, the mighty men, every slave and every free man, hid themselves in the caves and in the rocks of the mountains, and said to the mountains and rocks, "Fall on us and hide us from the face of Him who sits on the throne and from the wrath of the Lamb! For the great day of His wrath has come, and who is able to stand? (Revelation 6:12–17)

When He invited us to resurrection, we saw only the death that is the door through which we must pass to that resurrection. When He invited us to enjoy Him, we saw only that we must lose ourselves. He offers us Heaven, and we are too busy grasping this world with a death grip to appreciate the offer. And don't imagine that you and I aren't in that number for, as it says, "the kings, the great, the rich, the mighty, every slave and every free man." It is hard to find an exception to that set. This is the judgment: that we prefer our life, which is death, to the death of Christ, which is life, our darkness to His light.

There is a sort of understated irony that is very characteristic of the preaching of Jesus of Nazareth, which I find in the phrase "wrath of the Lamb." Although sheep are much more common in the Old World than they are in the American South, the

word used here is a little lamb, and the reference would have felt much the same to the first readers of this story as it does to us. There is a clear portrayal of passive helplessness, and of course Jewish readers would have felt the sacrificial tones of the word *lamb* quite as much as we do. What animal could be less inclined to show wrath than a little lamb? Of course, as John has already pointed out in chapter 5, this lamb is dead—dead to wrath and alive to grace. I don't know much about Greek, but it seems to me that there is another bit of irony in the word translated throughout Revelation as "wrath." When I was studying all of this, I became curious about this wrath and looked it up. It describes feelings so strong that they can't be contained. An alternate translation is "passion." Hide us from the Passion of Christ. When this was written, the end of Christ's life hadn't yet come to be called His Passion, as far as I can tell, but I think that that illustrates the problem we have with the apocalypse rather nicely. His way of salvation is a way that features a guilty verdict for us, suffering, death, and hell. It has all the external characteristics of wrath. It is only when you get inside that you can perceive it as passion, which, I think, is why, at the seventh seal, there is silence in Heaven. Christ has stooped down to open the knowledge of God to us, and we have made excuses not to take Him up on the offer. He set the scroll that is the Express Image of God right before us, and we were too attached to our own notions of who God is to take a look. It is the silence of shock and awe—not shock and awe, though, at our stubborn mistrust, but at the lengths which Christ is about to go to get guests at His party.[4]

> So that servant came and reported these things to his master. Then the master of the house, being angry, said to his servant, "Go out quickly into the streets and lanes of the city, and bring in here the poor and the maimed and the lame and the blind."
> (Luke 14:21)

The story proceeds to the blowing of seven trumpets. God is turning up the volume. Christ is done being refused by the religious set. He is now broadcasting the message of grace full volume. But how does He do that?

> The first angel sounded: And hail and fire followed, mingled with blood, and they were thrown to the earth. And a third of the trees were burned up, and all green grass was burned up.
>
> Then the second angel sounded: And something like a great mountain burning with fire was thrown into the sea, and a third of the sea became

---

[4] While I stand by what I have said about Wrath in this chapter, I wouldn't want it to be thought that I deny that the Lord makes use of wrath when He chooses, even everlasting wrath. What I do insist on is that wrath is never an end unto itself with the Lord, but is a shepherd's rod which produces repentance even with respect to the "wrath to come." I deal with this at greater length here: https://comfortwithtruth.substack.com/p/hell-and-damnation.

blood. And a third of the living creatures in the sea died, and a third of the ships were destroyed.

Then the third angel sounded: And a great star fell from heaven, burning like a torch, and it fell on a third of the rivers and on the springs of water. The name of the star is Wormwood. A third of the waters became wormwood, and many men died from the water, because it was made bitter.

Then the fourth angel sounded: And a third of the sun was struck, a third of the moon, and a third of the stars, so that a third of them were darkened. A third of the day did not shine, and likewise the night.

And I looked, and I heard an angel flying through the midst of heaven, saying with a loud voice, "Woe, woe, woe to the inhabitants of the earth, because of the remaining blasts of the trumpet of the three angels who are about to sound!" (Revelation 8:7-13)

This sounds like wrath. It sounds like judgment. But wrath and judgment are not ends unto themselves with God, but only means to His good pleasure, which is salvation. This is the story of God taking away the things that we depend on, the things that we think we need. Because, as He said of Jerusalem, "If you had known, even you, especially in this your day, the things that make for your peace! But now they are hidden from your eyes." (Luke 19:42) He burns the grass and the trees, He poisons the water both salt and fresh, He blots out the light of sun and moon. But it is only so that we will see that the Lamb is our Shepherd, only so that He can cause us to lie down in green grass beside the rivers of living water that issue from His throne. He blots out the sun because its light obscures the Light of the World. His judgment is to take away the things we imagine support and make us happy that we may perceive that He provides for us just as much without means of water and trees and the sun. Mercy doesn't merely triumph over judgment; mercy is the ground, the foundation on which judgment is built.

> Then I heard a loud voice from the temple saying to the seven angels, "Go and pour out the bowls of the wrath of God on the earth." So, the first went and poured out his bowl upon the earth, and a foul and loathsome sore came upon the men who had the mark of the beast and those who worshiped his image. Then the second angel poured out his bowl on the sea, and it became blood as of a dead man; and every living creature in the sea died. Then the third angel poured out his bowl on the rivers and springs of water, and they became blood. And I heard the angel of the waters saying:
>
> "You are righteous, O Lord,

The One who is and who was and who is to be,

Because You have judged these things.

For they have shed the blood of saints and prophets,

And You have given them blood to drink.

For it is their just due."

And I heard another from the altar saying, "Even so, Lord God Almighty, true and righteous are Your judgments." Then the fourth angel poured out his bowl on the sun, and power was given to him to scorch men with fire. And men were scorched with great heat, and they blasphemed the name of God who has power over these plagues; and they did not repent and give Him glory. Then the fifth angel poured out his bowl on the throne of the beast, and his kingdom became full of darkness; and they gnawed their tongues because of the pain. They blasphemed the God of heaven because of their pains and their sores, and did not repent of their deeds. Then the sixth angel poured out his bowl on the great river Euphrates, and its water was dried up, so that the way of the kings from the east might be prepared. And I saw three unclean spirits like frogs coming out of

the mouth of the dragon, out of the mouth of the beast, and out of the mouth of the false prophet. For they are spirits of demons, performing signs, which go out to the kings of the earth and of the whole world, to gather them to the battle of that great day of God Almighty.

"Behold, I am coming as a thief. Blessed is he who watches, and keeps his garments, lest he walk naked and they see his shame."

And they gathered them together to the place called in Hebrew, Armageddon. Then the seventh angel poured out his bowl into the air, and a loud voice came out of the temple of heaven, from the throne, saying, "It is done!" And there were noises and thunderings and lightnings; and there was a great earthquake, such a mighty and great earthquake as had not occurred since men were on the earth. Now the great city was divided into three parts, and the cities of the nations fell. And great Babylon was remembered before God, to give her the cup of the wine of the fierceness of His wrath. Then every island fled away, and the mountains were not found. And great hail from heaven fell upon men, each hailstone about the weight of a talent. Men blasphemed God because

of the plague of the hail, since that plague was exceedingly great. (Revelation 16:1–21)

Then the master said to the servant, 'Go out into the highways and hedges, and compel them to come in, that my house may be filled. For I say to you that none of those men who were invited shall taste my supper.' (Luke 14:23–24)

And so, when we don't bother to look at God as He has revealed Himself in the Living Book which is Christ the Lamb, when we don't listen when His Gospel is shouted across the earth with the voice of the Archangel, He takes our choice out of the equation, He pours out the bowls in which chapter 15 says the wrath of God is finished on the condemned, the beast, and those who bear his mark, on the last, the least, the certainly lost. And when the wrath is finished, when there is no more condemnation in the bowls, there is still grace. Christ is righteous when He judges and makes war, righteous with the righteousness which makes us righteous. Death and hell are His under shepherds to lead us to life and resurrection.

Revelation is a book of unexpected good news, the good news that God's mercy seat is no longer locked up in the Holy of Holies but is going out over the whole earth with the thunder of the white horse's hooves. The Gospel, which was once whispered in Palestine, is proclaimed over the earth with the trumpeting voice of the Archangel. The cup of the wrath of God has not

ceased to be the cup of the wrath of God, but when our Saviour drank from that cup, it became the cup of the New Covenant, the communion of the saints, the holiest of Holy Grails, justification by grace alone through faith alone in Christ alone, which David describes saying, "Blessed is the man to whom the Lord does not impute his sins" (Psalm 32:2) It is this cup that He pours out on the black sheep, those dead in sin and rebellion, toiling away in Babylon at the throne of the beast. Our distrust and our guilty consciences make us see only wrath when God makes war and righteous judgment because we make war and condemn only out of hatred and fear, but He has subjected Creation to futility, bloody, destructive, miserable futility not out of hate, fear, or anger but in hope, hope of the joy that is set before Him and us, joy that is not beyond the cross but within the cross. He has confined us under sin and condemned us as the necessary first step in showing mercy. He kills and damns that He might raise and justify.

> Now I saw heaven opened, and behold, a white horse. And He who sat on him was called Faithful and True, and in righteousness He judges and makes war. His eyes were like a flame of fire, and on His head were many crowns. He had a name written that no one knew except Himself. He was clothed with a robe dipped in blood, and His name is called The Word of God. And the armies in heaven, clothed in fine linen, white and clean,

followed Him on white horses. Now out of His mouth goes a sharp sword, that with it He should strike the nations. And He Himself will rule them with a rod of iron. He Himself treads the winepress of the fierceness and wrath of Almighty God. And He has on His robe and on His thigh a name written:

KING OF KINGS AND LORD OF LORDS. (Revelation 19:11–16)

And he showed me a pure river of water of life, clear as crystal, proceeding from the throne of God and of the Lamb. In the middle of its street, and on either side of the river, was the tree of life, which bore twelve fruits, each tree yielding its fruit every month. The leaves of the tree were for the healing of the nations. And there shall be no more curse, but the throne of God and of the Lamb shall be in it, and His servants shall serve Him. They shall see His face, and His name shall be on their foreheads. There shall be no night there: They need no lamp nor light of the sun, for the Lord God gives them light. And they shall reign forever and ever. (Revelation 22:1–5)

CHAPTER 3
The War in Heaven

The Red Horse

Originally Preached February 1, 2020

BEFORE WE GET TO OUR TEXT FOR TODAY, I
want to say that, when dealing with dreams and visions, it is
definitely possible to be overly analytical. Such poetry is not
aimed at the rational mind, but at deeper and more primal parts
of us. So, at least to begin with, let's not focus on identifying the
characters or significance of the story. Let's not worry about the
timing of the events. Just try and feel the story.

> Now a great sign appeared in heaven: a woman
> clothed with the sun, with the moon under her
> feet, and on her head a garland of twelve stars.
> Then being with child, she cried out in labor and
> in pain to give birth.
>
> And another sign appeared in heaven: behold, a
> great, fiery red dragon having seven heads and
> ten horns, and seven diadems on his heads. His
> tail drew a third of the stars of heaven and threw
> them to the earth. And the dragon stood before
> the woman who was ready to give birth, to devour
> her Child as soon as it was born. She bore a male
> Child who was to rule all nations with a rod of

iron. And her Child was caught up to God and His throne. Then the woman fled into the wilderness, where she has a place prepared by God, that they should feed her there one thousand two hundred and sixty days.

And war broke out in heaven: Michael and his angels fought with the dragon; and the dragon and his angels fought, but they did not prevail, nor was a place found for them in heaven any longer. So, the great dragon was cast out, that serpent of old, called the Devil and Satan, who deceives the whole world; he was cast to the earth, and his angels were cast out with him.

Then I heard a loud voice saying in heaven, "Now salvation, and strength, and the kingdom of our God, and the power of His Christ have come, for the accuser of our brethren, who accused them before our God day and night, has been cast down. And they overcame him by the blood of the Lamb and by the word of their testimony, and they did not love their lives to the death. Therefore rejoice, O heavens, and you who dwell in them! Woe to the inhabitants of the earth and the sea! For the devil has come down to you, having great wrath, because he knows that he has a short time."

Now when the dragon saw that he had been cast to the earth, he persecuted the woman who gave birth to the male Child. But the woman was given two wings of a great eagle, that she might fly into the wilderness to her place, where she is nourished for a time and times and half a time, from the presence of the serpent. So, the serpent spewed water out of his mouth like a flood after the woman, that he might cause her to be carried away by the flood. But the earth helped the woman, and the earth opened its mouth and swallowed up the flood which the dragon had spewed out of his mouth. And the dragon was enraged with the woman, and he went to make war with the rest of her offspring, who keep the commandments of God and have the testimony of Jesus Christ. (Revelation 12:1–17)

War in Heaven. The very idea touches something deep inside us. It feels as if the heavens should be perfect, that the wars and difficulties that trouble mankind should not reach to Heaven. When I hear this story, I want to ask, "Who would dare to bring war to Heaven? And why?" We aren't given a lot of background for this story, but the first thing that I would say is that the text we just read is the only source of information about this war. There are other passages of scripture that are sometimes thought to refer to Satan's fall, or to him as an angel, but the only time that this story is deliberately dealt with in scripture instead of sort of a passing reference is right here before us, so this is where we need to look for our answers. We shouldn't build a story with inferences from somewhere else and then try to fit Revelation 12 into our prebuilt scenario.

So, in the text, Michael is the aggressor. Telling this story, for me at least, begins with a whole lot of caveats, and here is the next bit of throat clearing. Michael is a rather mysterious character. He appears, I think, a total of four times in the Bible, and on his rather unknown shoulders a lot of angelology has been built up. Books have been written about who he is, what armies he commands, his history, his future. He has been represented in countless artworks and prayed to by almost every branch of the church. On the other hand, going back (at least) to Calvin's commentary on the prophet Daniel and extending through various arms of the faith, there is a suspicion that perhaps this is another name for Christ. To me, there is only one reason to spend as much time as I already have on the question of his identity. I simply bring it up to make the point that it doesn't matter. In the long run, the question of whether something is done by the physical body of Christ or some member of the mystical Body of Christ, the Church, is meaningless. (And while I don't intend to claim any great knowledge of the holy angels, I do deny that there is any holiness anywhere that is not derived from being "in Christ." Whatever our connection with these beings, they are to some extent brothers and sisters.) Something done by Jesus of

Nazareth is the same as something done by Dennis (a member of my original audience), in whom the Spirit of Christ dwells. Whoever Michael is personally, what we need to know about him is simply what spirit is within him. It is irrelevant whether he is Christ personally or he is Christ sacramentally, as a member of the body of Christ. Those who are in communion with Christ are one with Him just as He and His Father are one. So, the main point, and it is to me at least a bit of a curve ball, is that the aggressor in the war in Heaven is Christ. I realize that, before the war started, the dragon made some threatening gestures towards the Child's mother. The dragon's intentions certainly seemed hostile, but as soon as the Child ascended to His Father's throne, Michael's angels fired the first shots. So, the big question: is Christ righteous when He starts a war?

What led up to this conflict? The classic answers about Satan arrogantly challenging God or being jealous of man are probably not far from the truth, but they are not supported by this text, and I think that they leave out the part of the story that is most important for us to know, so I leave them out. But the text does give us a reason.

> Then I heard a loud voice saying in heaven, "Now salvation, and strength, and the kingdom of our God, and the power of His Christ have come, for the accuser of our brethren, who accused them before our God day and night, has been cast down. (Revelation 12:10)

The one who was cast out spent all his time accusing the saints.

So Satan answered the Lord and said, "Does Job fear God for nothing? Have You not made a hedge around him, around his household, and around all that he has on every side? You have blessed the work of his hands, and his possessions have increased in the land. But now, stretch out Your hand and touch all that he has, and he will surely curse You to Your face!" (Job 1: 9–11)

Then he showed me Joshua the high priest standing before the Angel of the Lord, and Satan standing at his right hand to oppose him. And the Lord said to Satan, "The Lord rebuke you, Satan! The Lord who has chosen Jerusalem rebuke you! Is this not a brand plucked from the fire?" Now Joshua was clothed with filthy garments, and was standing before the Angel. Then He answered and spoke to those who stood before Him, saying, "Take away the filthy garments from him." And to him He said, "See, I have removed your iniquity from you, and I will clothe you with rich robes." And I said, "Let them put a clean turban on his head." So they put a clean turban on his head, and they put the clothes on him. And the Angel of the Lord stood beside him. (Zechariah 3:1–5)

When Judah came back from captivity in Babylon, they were led by two men: Zerubbabel, the heir to the throne of David, and Joshua, the high priest.[5] Joshua is called here a brand plucked from the fire, and we have a picture of him being clothed in the righteousness of Christ. He was a lost soul, lost in his sins pictured by his filthy clothes, born in Babylon, the epitome of a place under the curse of God. His life was burning with sinfulness and the wrath that hung over him. But he was plucked from that fire, taken from a poor, enslaved exile to be the priest of the living God and to dwell in His House, clothed in pure linen, clean and white, the righteousness of the saints given to him graciously. Satan's accusations against him aren't recorded, but they don't really need to be do they? We can easily imagine what we would accuse him of, and that must be the sorts of things Satan accused him of. No doubt he had broken the law in many points. He was born and raised in Babylon. All his notions of righteousness would have fallen far below our idea of what the Law requires, far below Satan's idea of what righteousness is. Satan opposed this man being gratuitously allowed into communion with God.

And now I need to break off a little because I need to talk about our cartoon supervillain notions of Satan. God has no opposite. There is no personification of evil. Everyone acts out of what he or she believes is good. Evil comes from wrong ideas of what is good.

---

[5] I want just briefly to note that this is not the more famous Joshua, son of Nun, who was Moses' protégé and led the conquest of Canaan about whom the book of Joshua tells.

All sins come from wrong ideas of what is good. Selfishness, to take a simple example, is simply equating what we want with what is good. So, what is Satan's wrong idea of what is good? His idea is that people and things that aren't good should be quarantined from the righteous, especially from God. And that quarantine, which can never make the sinners clean, turns into a giant garbage dump, the never-ending tire fire landfill outside of Jerusalem, which is the archetype of hell. This idea of goodness sounds a lot like the Law or at least with the way that I have always understood it. The Accuser goes hand in hand with the "handwriting that was against us" (Colossians 2:14), and his being cast down with the erasing of that handwriting.

I suspect that angels and heavenly creatures are not personal and separate in the way that we think that they are. If we are members of Christ and members of one another, then that at least suggests that existence is not the disconnected, individual thing that we perceive it to be. I guess what I am getting at is that it seems to me that a lot of angels are or at least are intimately connected with what we call ideas or beliefs or dreams or hopes or fears. And the angel of the Law must be a very chief sort of angel, an archangel if you like that term, exactly as the rumors suggest the devil once was. How can I equate the Law which is holy and just and good, with the devil?

> For the creation was subjected to futility, not
> willingly, but because of Him who subjected it
> in hope; because the creation itself also will be

delivered from the bondage of corruption into the glorious liberty of the children of God. (Romans 8:20–21)

It doesn't say that humanity was subjected to futility or that Earth was subjected to futility. Our text today is the obvious proof that Heaven and the celestial beings have been subjected to futility. "The Creation" was subjected to futility—the whole creation. Just to be clear, the Creation means everything that has been created, which is another way of saying everything except the Creator Himself, which includes angels and—drumroll please—the Law. However good, and holy, and just, however perfect the Law is, we have one question that we must ask about it. Is the Law God? If the answer is no, then it has been subjected to futility, the Law as we know it, even the Law as delivered by a man inspired by the spirit of God, even the Law as written on tablets of stone with the burning finger of God, is in the same sinking boat as the rest of us, which strongly implies that it is not the solution to our problems. And what is true of the Law is also true of its angel.

But how is the Law, which is true, equated with the liar? We often assume that the way things are now is the way that they have always been. And it is generally believed that Satan fell before the creation of man. But that isn't what the Revelation of Jesus Christ says. It places the war as occurring shortly after the Lord's ascension, the Child's ascension to the throne of God. And to understand this text and understand our world, we must realize that the very foundations the world was built on were unmoored when the Child put His little flock of the last, the lost, and the least in possession of the entire kingdom of Heaven. In Job and Zechariah, there is no suggestion that Satan is at all unwelcome in Heaven or before the throne of God. When he accuses Joshua, the high priest, we hear a very restrained reply: "The Lord who has chosen Jerusalem rebuke you" (Zechariah 3:1). Civility might be strained, but it is maintained. Satan has a place and a role in Heaven, or at least he did. The angel of the Law must have had a rather depressing life. He went out going to and fro upon the earth, searching, hunting for a righteous man, and he never found one. He jealously protected the purity and righteousness of God by keeping all sinners far from Him. He kept us in our filthy clothes out of the clean, bright City of God. But the whole time he was a liar, although no one could see it.

Satan is the accuser, and all his accusations against us are true. Every time he calls me a sinner, he is dead on. He is a liar, but no one knows that he is lying because the things he is saying happen to be true. It seems confusing. But what it all comes down to is that he doesn't accuse me of being a sinner because it is true. It just happens to be true. It all went fine until he accused the Innocent Man. Keeping sinners like you and me separate from God seems eminently reasonable, but the Law condemned Christ and demanded that His Father forsake Him. The legal theory of purity, of holiness, hinges on keeping all the sinners locked up, and it marks us all as sinners. But when the accuser accused Christ, he tipped his hand. Although his accusations against us

are true, he never made them because they were true. If it had been about truth, he wouldn't have accused the Righteous Man. The Law has become futile. It can make us conscious of our failure, and it can mark us as sinners, but that is the extent of its power. It cannot make sinners righteous. The Law should be a happy thing, keeping good people on the right track, but having no good people to work with and being unable to help people like you and me, it became sick, it became darkened, and it had to go. So, the whole concept of keeping sinners away from God has been rejected. The purity that avoids all contact with the impure has been replaced with a purity that makes the impure pure, with a Messiah who touches lepers and makes them clean.

When Adam sinned, it wasn't just he and his children who fell. Everything fell with him. Maybe the angels and the better natures understood what was happening and submitted willingly to this strange prelude to the Revelation of divine grace, and maybe they didn't. But they fell either way. The Law is called holy and just and good, but no created thing can be holy and just and good in and of itself, and when a part of creation thinks that it is good on its own, then it is a wicked liar. The Father of Lies is the one who thinks he is righteous apart from Christ. I proved earlier that the Law is fallen and become futile by the fact that it is not the Creator, that all things besides Him are fallen, but when everything else had fallen, the Creator Himself descended lower than any of them. He placed Himself under the Law, under the self-righteous ones, under the criminals, even under the earth so

that He might place all things on His shoulders, like a little lost lamb on the shoulders of the Good Shepherd, and bear us with Him when He returned to His Father and Our Father. However good and holy a thing is, like the Law or however evil and dirty a thing is, like the devil, all must come to the One who is full of grace and truth, and all are called. The angel flies over the entire earth crying out the everlasting Gospel: "The Spirit and the bride say, 'Come!' And let him who hears say, 'Come!' And let him who thirsts come. Whoever desires, let him take the water of life freely" (Revelation 22:17).

Finally, let's look at how the war was fought and won. They, identified earlier as Michael's angels, overcame him by the blood of the Lamb, and the word of their testimony, and they did not love their lives to the death. I don't know a lot about angels, but that sounds like the apostles and martyrs of the church militant, the church on this earth, at war with the world, the flesh, and, yes, the devil. Satan has been defeated and cast out of Heaven by the exact same weapons and tactics that we are given that are called mighty for casting down strongholds and everything that exalts itself against the knowledge of God. What is the flaming archangel's sword that wins the war? What is the sword of the rider of the red horse who takes peace from the Earth? It is the Word of God, the truth that Christ is righteous though not according to our ideas of righteousness—righteous when He judges and when He makes war. The great weapons of our warfare are our testimonies—the testimony that, though

we are sinful men still, that we are Michael's angels, messengers of the Heavenly Prince entrusted with the ministry of gracious reconciliation. Our testimony is that we are brands plucked from the fire, like Joshua, still liable to all the accusations of the futile interpretation of the Law that our minds and Satan's produce, but righteous by the divine declaration of the angel of the Lord who clothes us in His own righteousness. And, as usual with Revelation, the instrument of our glorification is our death, and acceptance of that death. To not love our lives to the death unites us with the death of Christ, to hate our lives and welcome the return of the God who kills and makes alive is our victory. Woe to the inhabitants of the earth and the sea because Satan has come to them in great wrath. But the good news is that, though we appear to be inhabiting Earth it isn't true. Your reality and mine is that we are hidden in God with Christ, a reality that we can't see with our eyes but can hear in the preaching of the Gospel and feel and taste in the communion of the saints.

CHAPTER 4
No Rest for the Wicked

The Pale or Green Horse: Death

Originally preached Feb 2, 2020

Then a third angel followed them, saying with a loud voice, "If anyone worships the beast and his image, and receives his mark on his forehead or on his hand, he himself shall also drink of the wine of the wrath of God, which is poured out full strength into the cup of His indignation. He shall be tormented with fire and brimstone in the presence of the holy angels and in the presence of the Lamb. And the smoke of their torment ascends forever and ever; and they have no rest day or night, who worship the beast and his image, and whoever receives the mark of his name."

Here is the patience of the saints; here are those who keep the commandments of God and the faith of Jesus. Then I heard a voice from heaven saying to me, "Write: 'Blessed are the dead who die in the Lord from now on.'" "Yes," says the Spirit, "that they may rest from their labors, and their works follow them." (Revelation 14:9–13)

SO, WHAT I WANT TO TALK ABOUT TODAY IS REST.

I think that most of us want rest, but we can't seem to get it. I suppose that our text today is the source of the saying no rest for the wicked, and that's a pretty good summary of the first part of the passage we read. "They have no rest day or night" it says about God's enemies. It also mentions them being tormented, and that word *torment* suggests not so much being locked up in the torture chamber as it does hard labor, a job that is irksome, irritating, that makes you miserable. One other issue, before we move on, with the way our text reads is with the torment of the wicked occurring "in the presence" of the holy angels and in the presence of the Lamb. The word translated "in the presence" is *enopion*, which has the same root as our words *optics* and *optical* and is literally "in the eyes of." It is often used exactly the way that we use the phrase "in God's eyes" (or someone else's eyes) in English. In the New Testament, this word is used to contrast something being one way in the eyes of God and another in the eyes of men.[6] And I can't help but wonder if there is some of that here. Whenever we hear about the suffering of the damned in scripture, we are hearing about it from the point of view of the Lamb and the saints—in their eyes. But I suspect that it might look different to the ones who are doing this hard, unending, tormenting labor. We imagine that the work with which we have

---

[6] For example, here is Christ using the word when speaking to the Pharisees: "And He said to them, 'You are those who justify yourselves before men, but God knows your hearts. For what is highly esteemed among men is an abomination in the sight of God'" (Luke 16:15).

filled up our lives is purposeful and meaningful and that the slavery that characterizes our lives is the way that good people live their lives. And the Lamb and the saints look on in pity wandering how to show us what we are missing, searching for words that will convince us of the rest that God has in store for us if we will only put our labors away.

> God, who at various times and in various ways spoke in time past to the fathers by the prophets, has in these last days spoken to us by His Son, whom He has appointed heir of all things, through whom also He made the worlds; who being the brightness of His glory and the express image of His person, and upholding all things by the word of His power, when He had by Himself purged our sins, sat down at the right hand of the Majesty on high. (Hebrews 1:1–3)

God is not engaged in continual labor. He is not always working. He sat down. He wrapped it all up. Moses says that, on the seventh day, He rested, but actually Jesus said, "It is finished" and knocked off Friday at about three, which is a very good example to follow. Jammed right into the middle of His Law, shoved into the face of all of us who seek our own righteousness, is the Sabbath, the express image of God thumbing His nose in our faces, trying to wake us up to the rest we are missing. And don't let the characterization of the "wicked" following the beast and what not fool you. Seeking righteousness is exactly what they

are doing. They are working 24/7 at being good parents, good husbands, good human beings, going ninety miles an hour the wrong way down a one-way street.

Therefore, as the Holy Spirit says: "Today, if you will hear His voice, do not harden your hearts as in the rebellion, In the day of trial in the wilderness, where your fathers tested Me, tried Me, and saw My works forty years. Therefore, I was angry with that generation, and said, 'They always go astray in their heart, and they have not known My ways.' So, I swore in My wrath, 'They shall not enter My rest.'"

Beware, brethren, lest there be in any of you an evil heart of unbelief in departing from the living God; but exhort one another daily, while it is called "Today," lest any of you be hardened through the deceitfulness of sin. For we have become partakers of Christ if we hold the beginning of our confidence steadfast to the end, while it is said:

"Today, if you will hear His voice, do not harden your hearts as in the rebellion."

For who, having heard, rebelled? Indeed, was it not all who came out of Egypt, led by Moses? Now with whom was He angry forty years? Was it not

with those who sinned, whose corpses fell in the wilderness? And to whom did He swear that they would not enter His rest, but to those who did not obey? So, we see that they could not enter in because of unbelief. (Hebrews 3:7–19)

Rebellion is met with wrath and death and the inability to rest. So, those awful rascals who bear the mark of the beast get the same treatment as who? As the Children of Israel who followed Moses out of Egypt. And what is the sin that is being pointed out to us by their example? We become partakers of Christ if we hold the beginning of our confidence unchanged to the end as the text says. And those who do not do this are accused of unbelief. The beginning of our confidence is simply the unmerited favor of Christ. We begin confessedly unworthy, appealing for mercy based on His goodness not our deservingness. And then, after a while, we think maybe His goodness is missing a little around the edges. We think that there are things that we need to do to complete Christ's work. I mean, He should have at least kept going right up until sundown and the legal beginning of the Sabbath rather than quitting at three yelling "It's five o'clock somewhere" even if He was gonna take Saturday off, shouldn't He? He sat down and left us this whole kingdom to build, this whole world to win, all this work to do. So, we see that we cannot enter in because of unbelief. We cannot rest because we refuse to believe that our righteousness and our goodness are entirely superfluous; in fact, they are obstacles as much as

anything can be an obstacle to the relentless, furious, saving love of God.

Our lives of works and worthiness are the problem—all the things that we are trying to contribute to add on top of the works that were finished at the foundation of the world. What then is the solution?

> Here is the patience of the saints; here *are* those who keep the commandments of God and the faith of Jesus. Then I heard a voice from heaven saying to me, "Write: 'Blessed are the dead who die in the Lord from now on.'" "Yes," says the Spirit, "that they may rest from their labors, and their works follow them." (Revelation 14:12–13)

The solution is to die. To stop contributing, stop adding to the work of Christ, stop using our fig leaves to accessorize His pure, unalloyed, unmixed, goodness clean and white. It's not just okay to give up; it's commanded. The only thing that is required of us is something that all of us can do—die.

> But Christ came as High Priest of the good things to come, with the greater and more perfect tabernacle not made with hands, that is, not of this creation. Not with the blood of goats and calves, but with His own blood He entered the Most Holy Place once for all, having obtained eternal redemption. For if the blood of bulls and goats

and the ashes of a heifer, sprinkling the unclean, sanctifies for the purifying of the flesh, how much more shall the blood of Christ, who through the eternal Spirit offered Himself without spot to God, cleanse your conscience from dead works to serve the living God? And for this reason, He is the Mediator of the new covenant, by means of death, for the redemption of the transgressions under the first covenant, that those who are called may receive the promise of the eternal inheritance. (Hebrews 9:11–15)

The Old Covenant said that the man who keeps the Law shall live by the Law. And no one kept the Law, and so all died without that covenant providing the promised inheritance, the promised rest. The New Covenant doesn't fail because, by means of death, we receive life; by means of failure, we become more than conquerors; by means of condemnation, we are justified. Our life, which in the eyes of God is really death, is replaced by the death of Christ, which is truest life. Our righteous works, which in the eyes of God are sin, are replaced by the rest of Christ, an idleness that powerfully upholds all things. Our accomplishments are buried in the depths of the sea, and we obtain rest.

For where there is a testament, there must also of necessity be the death of the testator. For a testament is in force after men are dead, since it has no power at all while the testator lives. Therefore

not even the first covenant was dedicated without blood. For when Moses had spoken every precept to all the people according to the law, he took the blood of calves and goats, with water, scarlet wool, and hyssop, and sprinkled both the book itself and all the people, saying, "This is the blood of the covenant which God has commanded you." Then likewise he sprinkled with blood both the tabernacle and all the vessels of the ministry. And according to the law almost all things are purified with blood, and without shedding of blood there is no remission.

Therefore it was necessary that the copies of the things in the heavens should be purified with these, but the heavenly things themselves with better sacrifices than these. For Christ has not entered the holy places made with hands, which are copies of the true, but into heaven itself, now to appear in the presence of God for us; not that He should offer Himself often, as the high priest enters the Most Holy Place every year with blood of another— He then would have had to suffer often since the foundation of the world; but now, once at the end of the ages, He has appeared to put away sin by the sacrifice of Himself. And as it is appointed for men to die once, but after this the

judgment, so Christ was offered once to bear the sins of many. To those who eagerly wait for Him He will appear a second time, apart from sin, for salvation. (Hebrews 9:23–28)

CHAPTER 5
The Children Get Up and Reign

Resurrection

Originally preached July 5, 2020

A FEW WEEKS AGO, WHILE I WAS VISITING MY
dad, we decided to go and see his mother's grave since I had not
been there since her funeral. Cemeteries always hit me in a weird
place; I don't know how to describe what I think or feel when I
am there. But Carpenter Cemetery affects me most of all because
that is where my people are buried. It is just a field deep in rural
Florida. I think the land for it must have been part of a farm
before because it is still surrounded by fields with just a small
wild growth around to separate the cemetery from the farmland.
There is no church nearby; it is just a well-tended lawn with a few
bushes and a lot of curious stonework stuck in the ground. The
kids had been cooped up in the van all morning, so while Daddy
and I were looking at the graves and talking about our people
who were there, we let them run about on the paths. But when
they wanted to play hide and seek, I had to tell them no because
I didn't want them getting wild, and I was concerned that their
game might be disrespectful.

And I think that was the germination of my thoughts. Who
would their behavior be disrespectful to? Well, to the ones who
were in the graves. To the dead. To Granny and to her daddy,

whom I never met, and to Great Gran, who we buried the first time I was in that place when I was just a boy? But these weren't some anonymous, faceless dead whose presence called for an anonymous, faceless respect. They were people whom I knew, people who were planted there as seeds in the hope of rising again. And, as I thought about who they really were, it occurred to me that they would not be upset at children playing around their graves, and then I saw for a moment the dead rising, not as we had planted them but as children able to see the truth of the graveyard where they had lain for so long, able to see that it would be an excellent place to play hide and seek.

> Then I saw a great white throne and Him who sat on it, from whose face the earth and the heaven fled away. And there was found no place for them. And I saw the dead, small and great, standing before God, and books were opened. And the dead were judged according to their works, by the things which were written in the books. The sea gave up the dead who were in it, and Death and Hades delivered up the dead who were in them. And they were judged, each one according to his works. (Revelation 20:11–13)

One of the great themes in Revelation is that things go the way you expect them to up to a point. All the ancient societies that we know anything about had a story like this, of men being judged

after their death according to their works. And Revelation follows the script. Until it doesn't.

A lot of groups within Christianity that seem very different on the surface have very deep similarities. I am thinking of the Church of Rome and the Dispensationalists. I know that in a lot of ways they are very different, but the similarity that I have in mind is that they both see grace and forgiveness as a sort of big exception to justice, which they consider a fundamental reality. The Dispensationalists go so far as to talk of Christ's Church and His New Covenant as existing in a "parenthesis"—of them being isolated things that have no effect on the rest of time and space which lives under the rigor of the Law. The Romanists, on the other hand, see God as defaulting to a works-based judgment and only being moved if some outside force—Mary or one of the saints—pleads in a specific instance for grace. Now, personally, I think that both are examples of how the God of Philosophy, the God built out of what seems right to man, has been substituted for the God of Scripture.

> And I saw the dead, small and great, standing before God, and books were opened. And *another book* was opened, which is the Book of Life. And the dead were judged according to their works, by the things which were written in the books. The sea gave up the dead who were in it, and Death and Hades delivered up the dead who were in them. And they were judged, each one according to his

works. Then Death and Hades were cast into the
lake of fire. This is the second death. And anyone
not found written in the Book of Life was cast into
the lake of fire. (Revelation 20:12–15 emphasis
mine)

The first series of books to be opened contains our works, which
record our righteousness and our sin. And when we have been
judged on that account, *another book* will be opened, a book
that tells nothing about what we have done or failed to do and
everything about what Christ has done for us. It is my opinion
that the English versions of verse 15 have been poorly written.
Every one of them. The *not* should be attached to *anyone* and not
attached to *written.* I believe it should read, "And no one found
written in the Book of Life was cast into the lake of fire." This
does not change the meaning of the words but greatly changes
the emphasis to take it from judgment to salvation.

Our sins and our virtues, if any, have been made irrelevant. In
John's vision, the books of our works are read into the record
and a verdict is reached about us based on those works, and then
something more basic, more fundamental steps in and revises the
verdicts based solely on the goodness of God.

Victor Hugo tells a story in *Les Misérables* about Louis Phillipe,
who was made king of France during the Revolution. After having
rejected all kings, the citizens found that they again wanted a
king, for a time, and they put a good man on the throne, a man

who was prouder of being a physician, a healer, than of being the heir to the House of Orleans. This was a king who would pull out his Gladstone bag and treat his servants. But though the French people wanted a king again, they did not give him very much power. Louis Phillipe was, in many ways, a figurehead, but one power that he had, and used, was the power to "revise" sentences that had been given to criminals; that is, if the king could find any ground for leniency, anything that the court had missed, he could reduce the sentence. And Louis would stay up late into the night searching for grounds for mercy, as he put it "disputing every inch of ground with the guillotine." That is a beautiful and captivating piece of history, but it is not what is happening at the judgment seat of God. All the reasons for mercy have already been dealt with; every excuse has been made for us when the books of our works and of the Law have been considered. The sentence of damnation has been fully weighed with the scales balanced as far towards mercy as there is any possible grounds for. And then there is *another book*, not of Law or of works because they have been fully considered already, not of mercy for one reason or another. Rather, it is a book of sovereign grace.

Paul draws the scenario rather more simply when he says that the writing which is against us has simply been erased. But in both cases, what is significant is that justice—not weak and corrupt human justice, but the perfection of divine justice—gives way before something older, something more fundamental. Justice is shown to be logically accidental to God's nature when it collides with goodness and grace, which are shown to be of the essence of God. Mercy triumphs over justice, love covers a multitude of sins, and the Law not only cannot annul the promise that precedes it but, once it is fulfilled, the Law is annulled by the promise on which it is built.

We have tried to focus on the book of Revelation as "The Revelation of Jesus Christ," and we have seen Him righteous in judgment and when He makes war and holds the keys to death and hell, but I think that here we have the beginning and end of John's vision of Christ. The book begins with only the slain Lamb able to open the scroll, which I have said indicates that it is only through Christ's death that we can see the true nature of God, and almost the very end, after the wrath of God is finished, after the *krisis* of judgment in which God is shown as an impersonal law enforcer, the very idea of God that led Adam to hide behind the bush, "another book" is opened, the Tree of Life has been made into a Book of Life, and this is the revelation of Jesus Christ, the revelation of gracious salvation, that no one who is in the death of Christ is subject to his or her own death. His death is more alive than our lives.

> So also, is the resurrection of the dead. The body is sown in corruption, it is raised in incorruption. It is sown in dishonor, it is raised in glory. It is sown in weakness, it is raised in power. (1 Corinthians 15:42–43)

I remember my dead, and it is not that they had grown beyond play, that they had advanced to a sober mien and respectful deportment. And as I am becoming older and carrying myself in a little more dignified way myself, I recognize that this is not growth or advancement. We have not risen above play but fallen back from it as our bodies are no longer up to the task of play. I pray, however, that our hearts and our minds have not become so sick and frail as our bodies, and I know that my Granny's had not, and from what I remember of her mother, she had not either. And I dreamed them, risen as children, hiding behind gravestones and chasing one another around and over and through the graves they had vacated.

While I don't mean to say that we haven't made any progress from our childhood, much of what we have learned has been how to make do with reduced circumstances. We have learned how to eat and live to take care of bodies that once could consume nothing but colored sugar and run and jump all day long without the slightest twinge of pain or fatigue. We have learned how to get by in a world that provides only a scanty part of what we need mixed with great piles of futility.

> It is sown a natural body, it is raised a spiritual body. There is a natural body, and there is a spiritual body. And so it is written, "The first man Adam became a living being." The last Adam became a life-giving spirit.

However, the spiritual is not first, but the natural, and afterward the spiritual. The first man was of the earth, made of dust; the second Man is the Lord from heaven. As was the man of dust, so also are those who are made of dust; and as is the heavenly Man, so also are those who are heavenly. And as we have borne the image of the man of dust, we shall also bear the image of the heavenly Man. (1 Corinthians 15:44–49)

We have borne the image of Adam, and what is Adam's story? It is to begin with freedom and health and power and joy and to sink into slavery and sickness and frailty and misery. But we shall bear the image of Christ, and what is Christ's story? It is to triumph in and through all these things, a spirit whose life overflows so much that it brings life to all around. The problem with the world that we live in can be defined very simply. All the imagination and creativity and all the dreams are concentrated in the boys. And all the skill and the knowledge and the capability is concentrated in the men. By the time that we learn how to make things happen, we have forgotten the grand and noble things that we once wanted to make happen, and we use our skill and knowledge to make trivial and petty things happen instead. And so, greatness would be to obtain the skill and knowledge of manhood without losing the vision of boyhood, and I must insist that the resurrection is not a rising to an eternal choir practice or an eternal church service

but a new life, not simply being carried to a senior center of a Heaven, but to new heavens and a new Earth, new worlds to explore, new adventures to have, and the capacity to have and enjoy those adventures.

> Now this I say, brethren, that flesh and blood cannot inherit the kingdom of God; nor does corruption inherit incorruption. Behold, I tell you a mystery: We shall not all sleep, but we shall all be changed— in a moment, in the twinkling of an eye, at the last trumpet. For the trumpet will sound, and the dead will be raised incorruptible, and we shall be changed. For this corruptible must put on incorruption, and this mortal must put on immortality. So when this corruptible has put on incorruption, and this mortal has put on immortality, then shall be brought to pass the saying that is written: "Death is swallowed up in victory." "O Death, where is your sting? O Hades, where is your victory?" (1 Corinthians 15:50–55)

So, what does all this mean? What's the takeaway? Just that we shouldn't let the failure of this body be the failure of our dreams. So, I'm asking you simply to set goals and dream dreams that cannot be completed in this life. When this life is over, our accomplishments will be meager, our contribution insignificant, and if, in this life only, we have hope, then we are truly pitiful. So, the book of human wisdom advises us to set goals consistent with

the tight constraints we live under. But there is *another book*, and it promises that what we can do now compares to the glory that will be revealed in us, as a seed compares to a tree. Don't let the end of this life be the end of your dreams.

INTERLUDE
Omega Male

Originally Preached December 2016

GROWING UP IN A SMALL-TOWN FUNDAMENTALIST church in the Deep South, the "end times" were always being talked about and thought about. We were devoutly committed to the pretribulation, premillennial, futurist vision of God raining down punishment on all the people who did the things that we weren't free to do and giving us bigger and better versions of the few things that we were allowed to enjoy, mostly ruling over others and being spiritually rich. I heard the views of our microscopic clique defended as the very Word of God and treated as if it were impossible for anyone who knew God to come up with any other conclusion when reading the strangest, most mysterious piece of literature ever written. Of course, we didn't really recognize John's apocalypse as mysterious, poetic, and certainly not literary; in fact, my mathematician grandfather wrote a book explaining all of the numbers in Revelation as if it were as straightforward as arithmetic and proving beyond all doubt that the "tribulation" would begin in 1993 and the Lord would return in 2000 to set up a government in Jerusalem.

My childhood seems pretty bizarre looking back, but this view of the Lord's return is deeply entrenched in Christianity. We were willing to excommunicate over the details of our eschatological scheme, and it seems as if no one ever questioned the big picture of Jesus Christ as the ultimate Alpha Male. Now, in a certain sense, no one should question that picture. He spoke the worlds into existence. He stared Adam down and judged the whole of humanity with all the authoritativeness of the most type-A CEO imaginable. He wiped the slate clean in a flood that forever changed the face of the earth and arbitrarily chose Abram from the rest of the idolaters as never a revolutionary dictator reshaped his country. He got straight in Pharaoh's face and dragged several million people, kicking and screaming, from the slave pens of Egypt like the greatest comic book Superman ever, and then He proceeded to regulate the smallest details of their lives from a burning, storming mountain with unimaginable tyranny. This is a true picture of Christ, the Lord who never changes. But it isn't the only picture of Him.

I long ago rejected the theories of God that imagine some discontinuity between the God of Genesis and Exodus and the Christ of the Gospels. Christ must be the same both in Eden and Gethsemane, legislating from Sinai, and preaching the Sermon on the Mount, walking the forty years in the desert and walking the Via Dolorosa else He is not Himself. But the two pictures seem so radically different that it is hard—maybe impossible—for our minds to combine them into a single, consistent picture. What two things could seem more opposite than Joshua conquering Palestine city by city, terrifying the

inhabitants with divine might and disposing of all things as he chose, and the Apostles chased from city to city, laughingstocks and the butt of jokes, in prison, on the execution block, helpless and foolish. As I grow older, I have become more respectful of those who, seeing this difficulty, simply throw up their hands and exclaim that this must be the work of two different gods. At least they are taking an honest look and choosing an option that seems credible rather than defending something that they think ridiculous simply out of fear that rejecting it will exclude them from the love of God. Is there a combination of the two in which we can rest? Can the firstborn of all creation be the last and least of men, rejected and despised? Can the Alpha of all Alphas be Omega?

It seems as if we are stuck with a picture that we can't get into focus. All the lines seem blurred like a photo of a moving object. And I think that is the problem. We see a snapshot at one moment in time of that which is outside time, the Eternal One. He never moves, and He always moves. From the beginning, He works, but His whole being is a Sabbath rest. To begin to understand Him, we need that snapshot, but we also need a video and a narrative. To tell a story, though, we are going to need more than one character. The other character in our story is made from the dust, the lowest and humblest imaginable. His life is lived in the very dust from which He came, toiling dragging his living from the soil. He is a murderer, a madman, a thief, and a liar. It is fair to say that he has "sought out many schemes" (Ecclesiastes

7:29) which have turned Earth from a paradise into a hell. Every advance we have made has proven to simply be ways to increase the mayhem we cause. This man "made in the image of God" seems more like a photographic negative, and as God is all light, we seem to be all darkness. And that is the problem that causes the plot of our story. Like all good stories, it is a love story; in our case a love story between one who is high and lifted up and one who is wallowing in his own filth.

It is the story, then, of a great prince in love with a peasant woman.[7] The glory of love is to make the unequal equal. And in our imagination, this can be done by raising the lower to the level of the higher, but reality is more glorious than that, and more serious than our childish stories. In the real world, the only way is for the greater to willingly making himself less that He and His love might be one. The prince then becomes a peasant, not just in appearance but in reality. Reality is that Cinderella doesn't move into the palace; happily ever after happens in a shack with the Prince digging ditches to put food on her table. He who previously owned the cattle of a thousand hills must now either work or starve, but to get closer to the matter, He who once said, "Your brother's blood cries out to me from the ground" (Genesis 4:10) must say "I am not a judge between you and your brother" (Luke 12:14 paraphrase). The

---

[7] This telling of His story owes much to S. Kierkegaard, particularly his amazing look at faith in the life of Abraham, *Fear and Trembling*, a difficult read but incredibly insightful.

wisdom which ordered all things is reduced to a simplicity that honest men find difficult to tell from retardation at times. I can't make this story as true as the Four Evangelists made it; somehow, they show Him as both at the same time, which is the truth and beyond my poor ability. We get that. He made Himself the lowest and least of men, but somehow, we think it was just a show and that, at the Ascension He became again what He was before. Such a thought is unworthy of Him. To do so would be for Him to go backwards. Paradoxically, even when He is most a man, He is not a man that He should repent. The great pattern of His story cannot be reversed; the Prince gets ever lower and lower. He was once all that is; by His choice He can now be trivialized, marginalized, overlooked.

The only thing that we can see lower than a baby in a stable, than a child who is a fugitive and exile, is a condemned man on a cross. But there is something yet lower. I don't know what it is because, despite it being almost twenty years after His predicted return, He has not shown it to us yet. Might I suggest, though, that His second coming will be yet more humiliating than His first and will cement Him to ourselves yet more surely? The glorious picture that John, the greatest of all poets, saw can be seen only by the poetic part of man. In our eyes, His return may be pathetic, laughable, and probably end yet more tragically than His life. But the question is, will your heart sing at the poetry of the Lord of Heaven and earth becoming literally garbage for the woman He loves?

Now when He had taken the scroll, the four living creatures and the twenty-four elders fell down before the Lamb, each having a harp, and golden bowls full of incense, which are the prayers of the saints. And they sang a new song, saying:

"You are worthy to take the scroll,

And to open its seals;

For You were slain,

And have redeemed us to God by Your blood

Out of every tribe and tongue and people and nation,

And have made us kings and priests to our God;

And we shall reign on the earth."

Then I looked, and I heard the voice of many angels around the throne, the living creatures, and the elders; and the number of them was ten thousand times ten thousand, and thousands of thousands, saying with a loud voice:

"Worthy is the Lamb who was slain

To receive power and riches and wisdom,

And strength and honor and glory and blessing!"

And every creature which is in Heaven and on the earth and under the earth and such as are in the sea, and all that are in them, I heard saying:

"Blessing and honor and glory and power

Be to Him who sits on the throne,

And to the Lamb, forever and ever!"

Then the four living creatures said, "Amen!" And the twenty-four elders fell down and worshiped Him who lives forever and ever. (Revelation 5:8–14)

CHAPTER 6
The Mount of Olives

The Glorious Appearing

Originally preached Dec 9, 2020

OPPOSITES ATTRACT. WHETHER IN PHYSICS OR
relationships or theology, this seems to hold true. Protons and
electrons know no peace until they find the one that completes
them. Like the elementary particles, we rush toward one who
seems most different from us, knowing that, if we can get close
enough, we can find that deeper union. We sense that the surface
differences arise from some fundamental and elementary fitness
for one another. This has kind of always been my guiding principle
for understanding the scriptures; that is, where I find the thing
that sticks out, that seems different, that is an opportunity to
find the deeper underlying unity. And the main goal of the study
of Revelation has been to see how the strange, wrathful, war-
making, mysterious Christ of John's visions really hasn't changed
since He walked and talked and loved and cried and died and
rose. He told His disciples that, if they searched the prophets,
they would find Him because He was the One the prophets wrote
about. I have been searching the New Testament prophet for the
same purpose—to find Christ and His Gospel.

Some might argue that I have ignored the obvious in my search,
that I have not so much found the Christ of Revelation as I have

twisted Him into the Christ of the Gospels. If I have, I have. But this conflict between Christ's love and His wrath is one of the fundamental difficulties of the Christian experience. And I can't pretend to resolve or even ease the difficulty that we all feel when we see our loving gentle Lamb being the Lion; in fact, it's not even my goal today to try. Instead, I intend to wake up the difficulty, to bring it to the front of your life for a few moments, to rub your nose in the fact that there is a very real and true side of Christ that you and I find very difficult to accept. If we wish to see these two sides of Christ, then, like everything about Him, they seem to get turned up to eleven when you throw Jerusalem into the mix.

Jesus had a continual attraction to Jerusalem for a lot of reasons that we can only partly understand—Zion; the Mount Moriah where He rescued Isaac; the City of David for which He rose up early again and again with Jeremiah to try and save; His Own that He came to and was rejected by. The City on the Seven Hills that stoned the Prophets and crucified Him both attracted and frustrated Him. The great love of His life, His one great passion, that stormiest of romances could wheel from "Hosanna to the Son of David" (Matthew 21:9) to "His blood be on us and on our children" (Matthew 27:25) in such a short space of time. When the Man of Sorrows wept, mostly He wept over Jerusalem's refusal to be loved by Him. Anyone who has loved knows what it is like when you can't stand to be away from your beloved, and if you have loved for long then you know that sometimes you can't stand to be around her either. The Lord experienced this with

Jerusalem. When, as often happened, He couldn't stand to be in Jerusalem but refused to be away from her, He had sort of a relief valve called the Mount of Olives. Over and over in the Gospels, we see Christ in Jerusalem seeking a rest from Jerusalem in His hidden place on Olivet. The Mount of Olives is one of the seven hills on which the city was built. It sort of supports the eastern side of the city, and many of its slopes offered a place of solitude while still being very near Jerusalem.

In the Gospels, when we find Jesus teaching the twelve apart from the crowd, I think that very often it was in this place. His habit of coming here was so pronounced that, when Judas sought Him, he led the soldiers here with no doubt in his mind that they would find Christ in His hidden garden on the mountain. But what does any of this have to do with Revelation? Because it is to this place that He is going to return.

> Behold, the day of the Lord is coming, and your spoil will be divided in your midst. For I will gather all the nations to battle against Jerusalem; The city shall be taken, the houses rifled, And the women ravished. Half of the city shall go into captivity, But the remnant of the people shall not be cut off from the city. Then the Lord will go forth and fight against those nations, As He fights in the day of battle. And in that day His feet will stand on the Mount of Olives, which faces Jerusalem on the east. (Zechariah 14:1–4)

However much we don't like to think about it, Jesus Christ is the Lord of Hosts, He is the One who leads us into battle. That's not something that is all in the past. The Lamb does not supersede the Lion; rather, He is both simultaneously. And the differences between the children of God and the nations of this world are not going to be settled amicably. We try to pretend otherwise; we hope otherwise. But when it comes down to a fight, as it inevitably will, know that the Lord is on our side.

> And the Mount of Olives shall be split in two,
> from east to west, making a very large valley; Half
> of the mountain shall move toward the north and
> half of it toward the south. (Zechariah 14:4)

Just a brief pause for those who think that maybe this is all in the past and relates to the Roman destruction of Jerusalem or something like that. If you aren't sure, just check Google Earth and see if the mountain has been split in two. See if there is a big valley with a river in it flowing out of the Eastern Gate of Jerusalem where the mountain used to be. If there ain't then I am pretty sure that Christ's return to Jerusalem is something still to look forward to.

> Then you shall flee through My mountain valley,
> for the mountain valley shall reach to Azal. Yes,
> you shall flee as you fled from the earthquake in
> the days of Uzziah king of Judah. Thus, the Lord
> my God will come, and all the saints with You. It

shall come to pass in that day that there will be no light; the lights will diminish. It shall be one day which is known to the Lord—neither day nor night. But at evening time it shall happen that it will be light. And in that day, it shall be that living waters shall flow from Jerusalem, half of them toward the eastern sea and half of them toward the western sea; In both summer and winter it shall occur.

And the Lord shall be King over all the earth. In that day it shall be— "The Lord is one," And His name one. All the land shall be turned into a plain from Geba to Rimmon south of Jerusalem. Jerusalem shall be raised up and inhabited in her place from Benjamin's Gate to the place of the First Gate and the Corner Gate, and from the Tower of Hananel to the king's winepresses. The people shall dwell in it; And no longer shall there be utter destruction, But Jerusalem shall be safely inhabited. (Zechariah 14:5–11)

This is the famous millennial reign when Christ rules the nations from Jerusalem. There is, in this text, no indication of allegory. While the passage is filled with meaning on many levels, it is definitely not merely symbolic.

And this shall be the plague with which the Lord will strike all the people who fought against Jerusalem: Their flesh shall dissolve while they stand on their feet, their eyes shall dissolve in their sockets, and their tongues shall dissolve in their mouths. It shall come to pass in that day that a great panic from the Lord will be among them. Everyone will seize the hand of his neighbor, and raise his hand against his neighbor's hand; Judah also will fight at Jerusalem. And the wealth of all the surrounding nations shall be gathered together: gold, silver, and apparel in great abundance. Such also shall be the plague on the horse and the mule, on the camel and the donkey, and on all the cattle that will be in those camps. So shall this plague be.

And it shall come to pass that everyone who is left of all the nations which came against Jerusalem shall go up from year to year to worship the King, the Lord of hosts, and to keep the Feast of Tabernacles. And it shall be that whichever of the families of the earth do not come up to Jerusalem to worship the King, the Lord of hosts, on them there will be no rain. If the family of Egypt will not come up and enter in, they shall have no rain; they shall receive the plague with which the Lord strikes the nations who do not come up to

keep the Feast of Tabernacles. This shall be the punishment of Egypt and the punishment of all the nations that do not come up to keep the Feast of Tabernacles.

In that day "HOLINESS TO THE LORD" shall be engraved on the bells of the horses. The pots in the Lord's house shall be like the bowls before the altar. Yes, every pot in Jerusalem and Judah shall be holiness to the Lord of hosts. Everyone who sacrifices shall come and take them and cook in them. In that day there shall no longer be a Canaanite [Palestinian] in the house of the Lord of hosts. (Zechariah 14:12–20)

This is not what is known in modern Middle Eastern politics as a "two state solution." Now we can hear more about this war and this millennium from Revelation, especially chapters 17 through 20. But I assume no one doubts that that is there, and I want to rush on to our main point, which is that, however the Lord's return looks, however much it might appear that He is going to be king over this world, the kingdom He preaches is *not* of this world and *never* will be.

In the Old Testament the Mount of Olives is mentioned only twice that I can find, once as we have read from Zechariah as the place to which Christ will return, and once, incidentally, as a place where David paused while fleeing from Absalom. But in the Gospels, this mountain takes on an importance, a centrality with regard to His return that only the presence and significance of His garden can account for. Christ's return is a return to the Mount of Olives, which I propose should be read first and foremost as a return to Gethsemane.

> Now as He sat on the Mount of Olives, the disciples came to Him privately, saying, "Tell us, when will these things be? And what will be the sign of Your coming, and of the end of the age?" (Matthew 24:3)

Christ's famous discourse on His return, the Olivet Discourse, the so-called Synoptic Apocalypse, where He gathered together all of the terrifying, upsetting signs and signals of His return, where He laid on the judgment as thick as He was able, was delivered in private to His disciples on the Mount of Olives, which means that, in all probability, it was delivered in the place where Judas was so confident that He could be found, the place where you and I have found Him time and again—Gethsemane. So, combine all that apocalyptic, judgmental imagery with the tortured faith of Our Lord in His Father's will. Combine, if you can, ruling the nations with a rod of iron with patiently awaiting the traitor's kiss. His return is not a new thing, but the completion of what Luke calls, "the decease [the death] He was about to accomplish at Jerusalem" (Luke 9:31). It is from this place that Christ ascended, and from this place, according to the first chapter in Acts, to which He will return. He does not return to condemn and strike

the wicked, but to deliver His people. The condemnation and striking are necessary but incidental accompaniments to that salvation.

His return is a response to the cry of the martyrs under the altar who say "How long, O Lord, until you avenge our blood?" (Revelation 6:10 paraphrase), for precious in the sight of the Lord is the death of His saints. This world's attachment to its own righteousness is fundamentally irreconcilable with the saints who do not justify themselves but hope that God will justify them as He indeed does by raising them up just as He raised up Christ.

CHAPTER 7
Come Quickly,
Lord Jesus

The Life of the World to Come

Originally preached Jan 9, 2021

SO, A STUDY OF REVELATION SHOULD END BY
talking about eternal life, about what our state will be when
God's mighty acts are completed, which is a bit of a stumper
since we don't—certainly I don't—know much of anything about
the future state. A much wiser, much more insightful, and much
more inspired man than I wrote:

> Beloved, now we are children of God; and it has
> not yet been revealed what we shall be, but we
> know that when He is revealed, we shall be like
> Him, for we shall see Him as He is. (1 John 3:2)

I personally think that John the Apostle is John of Patmos; that
is, the author of John's Gospel is the author of John's Epistles,
and also the author of the book of Revelation. I don't know it
for a fact, but I suspect it. Further, I think that the visions he
records in the Revelation, with the exception of the letters to
the seven churches, he had at a rather early date, probably in
the AD 40 decade, long before he wrote the epistle that we call
1 John (even if they were not placed into the form in which we
have received them until later in his life). I think that much of
what seems so different between John's writings and those of

the other apostles, and the Christology that critics say is much too advanced and developed for the first century, especially that found in his Gospel, is explained by years—decades more likely—of thinking about the Jesus that he saw in these visions recorded in the Revelation and looking for the unity between that Jesus and the Jesus that he walked around Galilee with in his youth. And the man who saw the throne room of Heaven, saw the New Jerusalem come down out of Heaven, saw the city that needs no sun for its light is the Lamb, said near the end of his life that it wasn't really clear to *him* what *we* shall be in that day. So, you can bet that I don't know.

So much focus is put on trying to bring us to eternal life, but it's an eternal life that is a big mystery to us. So, I want to look at it another way, in the light of John's comments that "seeing Christ as He is" will make us like him (1 John 3:2), and "this is eternal life, that they may know You, the only true God, and Jesus Christ whom You have sent" (John 17:3). So, our stated goal has been to reveal Christ, to bring men to the knowledge of Him, so I will attempt to recap what we have said about Christ, not merely as a conclusion, but as offering us the only knowledge about the next life, about who and what we will be, which can be meaningful to us in this life.

So, the story is about a scroll. That's how we began this journey almost two years ago—with the knowledge of God sealed in a scroll, a knowledge that must be opened to us not once, but seven times—that is to say continuously—by the slain Lamb.

The knowledge of God must never launch itself into exalted speculation but must be unceasingly grounded in the hill of Calvary. The knowledge of God is described either as four separate horsemen or as the four activities of the Rider of the White Horse. He is the Conqueror, who is righteous in judgement, and when He makes war. He is followed by death and hell, whose keys He holds and wields.

In what sense is He the Conqueror? We said that legalism is the placing of God in a box. It is limiting what He can or will do for us, such that we seek good from other sources—from our own knowledge, from an apple, from a snake. And so, the conquering Gospel is the news that the heavens cannot contain Him! All of creation is too small an arena for His grace to be fully unfurled, and He is sovereignly determined to be absolutely as good and gracious as can be, and so certainly no temple, no box, no statutes, no limitations on to whom or how or when he might be merciful can be stipulated. We are bound to ways and means, but His Gospel rides over the whole earth unimpeded. He is able to enter every pigpen, palace, or prison seeking His black sheep and lost coins. In short, the Rider of the White Horse may be said to always be riding down the Damascus Road, always taking us stubborn Sauls so zealous for the Law, so eager to persecute any who do not walk according to our traditions, always taking us and making us into Pauls. Thus, He irresistibly conquerors our rebel hearts. We, then, will be conquerors— more than conquerors as John has it in another place. We will

have the ability to bring the Gospel to bear in any situation, as Christ did to Saul, to transform our world by applying the power of His resurrection.

We looked at His judgments, specifically those which seem most abhorrent to us, His plagues. When we see Him raining fire on the Earth, destroying the trees and grasses, killing the fish and the animals, poisoning the water, and causing diseases on men, our fallen minds conclude that He is unrighteous. Yes, we ourselves conclude that He is unrighteous. But just and true are all His ways, and these plagues only take away the means, the signs of blessing and not the blessing itself. He separates us from those things on which we imagine we depend—water and food, the grasses and trees, all of those things which we imagine bring us good, peace, and health, which we imagine we need, life itself, so that we can see that He alone has always been the sole source of our good. If we lose all else and retain Christ, then we have lost nothing, and we have gained clarity. This absolutely applies to us. Paul tells us that we will judge angels and are certainly competent to judge earthly matters. In the resurrection, then, we will be able to do what men have been trying to do since the Fall to set the systems of society and the earth right. Utopia famously doesn't exist, and every attempt to create it has only led to hate and destruction. Every revolution has only been a swapping of one set of oppressors for another. But there is a time coming when He will rule the world from His holy mountain.

Now it shall come to pass in the latter days That the mountain of the Lord's house Shall be established on the top of the mountains, And shall be exalted above the hills; and peoples shall flow to it. Many nations shall come and say, "Come, and let us go up to the mountain of the Lord, to the house of the God of Jacob; He will teach us His ways, and we shall walk in His paths." For out of Zion the law shall go forth, and the word of the Lord from Jerusalem. He shall judge between many peoples, and rebuke strong nations afar off; They shall beat their swords into plowshares, and their spears into pruning hooks; nation shall not lift up sword against nation, neither shall they learn war anymore. But everyone shall sit under his vine and under his fig tree, and no one shall make them afraid; for the mouth of the Lord of hosts has spoken. For all people walk each in the name of his god, but we will walk in the name of the Lord our God forever and ever. "In that day," says the Lord, "I will assemble the lame, I will gather the outcast And those whom I have afflicted; I will make the lame a remnant, and the outcast a strong nation; so the Lord will reign over them in Mount Zion from now on, even forever and you, O tower of the flock, the stronghold of

the daughter of Zion, to you shall it come, even the former dominion shall come, the kingdom of the daughter of Jerusalem." (Micah 4:1–8)

We considered when Christ makes war. He makes war on those who accuse the saints, whether in Heaven or on the Earth. Though He waits for a long time, He will stand up for His martyrs and will show that, in the words of the prophets, His arm is not shortened (Isaiah 59:1). For our sake, He makes war on every idea, every angel, every power that is against His people and against the knowledge of the cross. Most of all, He makes war on the "handwriting that is against us." He makes war on law as it is understood by fallen hearts. He makes war on condemnation. He makes war on the whole system of the universe, when it proves itself, as it has, to be against Him and against His little flock. Christ makes war on the Law exactly by placing himself under it. He makes war on the Law by being killed by it and being justified against it when God raises Him not merely from the grave but to the right hand of His Father.

But He has placed Himself not merely under Law but under death and under hell. All the things which condemn us are themselves condemned because they have condemned Christ, who is not merely undeserving of condemnation but is the Lord of Glory. But they have been more than condemned; they have been conquered as completely as Saul of Tarsus. Death is condemned for raising its hand against Jesus but is delivered from the futility to which it has been subjected to become the vehicle of resurrection. He

has descended beneath all things that He might raise all things up with Him.

Law is confronted by something more primal, more basic than itself. Mercy triumphs over justice in the way that the foundation triumphs over the superstructure. And when all the books of our works are opened and speak condemnation to us, they are silenced by *another book*—by the book of the true and living Lamb. And though we have grown old in the ways of this world, we will be made children again in His resurrection. Though we have grown wise in evil and suffering, we will be innocent and simple once more. There are new heavens and a new Earth, an abiding home for us, a city with foundations., which Abel and Abraham and all our fathers before us have preferred to seek as pilgrims rather than live in this world as their home. If we didn't feel like strangers and pilgrims in this world previously, then recent events have made it painfully clear that we will never belong here. Our home has been far away, invisible; it has been the stuff of dreams, but it will not be so much longer.

Our beloved is returning soon—the very same Jesus who loved us and gave Himself for us. He is returning unchanged, returning in and through the way of the cross. His feet shall stand again on the Mount of Olives, shall again walk the paths of Gethsemane. His return is a response to the cry of the martyrs under the altar who say "How long, O Lord, until you avenge our blood?" For precious in the sight of the Lord is the death of His saints. This world's attachment to its own righteousness is fundamentally irreconcilable with the saints who do not justify themselves but hope that God will justify them as He indeed does by raising them up just as He raised up Christ. The great tension between faith and works must end, and it ends in blood, it ends with works being cast into the lake of fire that there may be rest. The Lord has seen that all creation needs its rest, its sabbaths, and since we continue to deprive ourselves and our world of that rest by our obsession with justifying ourselves by our works, He will put an end to all works. Human effort and the worship of that beast is overcome by the Lord who would not fight the soldiers who came to take Him but healed the ear that Peter cut. As horrible as a face-melting plague sounds (Zechariah 14:2–3), it can, like all authority in Heaven and Earth, be trusted to the One who gave Himself for us. The fundamental issue we need to see about the Lord's return is not when or how, but who and where, so that, whatever attends the return, we can see it is the return of the Beloved in and through the way of the cross. We may then say with real feeling, "Even so, Come quickly Lord Jesus" (Revelation 22:20).

AFTERWORD

Thank you for reading my book. The Lord called and separated me to His Gospel, not in the generic way that many are called but specifically to "Speak comfort to Jerusalem, and cry out to her, That her warfare is ended, That her iniquity is pardoned; For she has received from the Lord's hand Double for all her sins" (Isaiah 40:2).

All my efforts in ministry are directed to that goal, to bring comfort to the Lord's people, to give them rest from their warfare, and as I say in the dedication of this book, I have sought to give rest from fear of the Lord's return and the accompanying "tribulation" to all of His people through this book, but especially to my children. The problem that we have with His Gospel is that the parts that are comforting do not appear to be comforting; they seem terrifying, like condemnation and death. The way to do Christian ministry is to first seek out the truth, to declare it as plainly as possible, and then to search within that truth for comfort; it is never to seek comfort and then hope that what you think is comfort is true.

If you have made it this far, there is a good chance that you would like to read more of my work. It is available at comfortwithtruth. substack.com. We are giving out one-year subscriptions with proof of purchase of this book (a picture of a receipt or other proof). I hope to see you there.

Love and peace,

—jc

About the Author

Jonathon Cutchins is an engineer by trade, separated to Christ's Gospel at nineteen. He's been sharing the Gospel through his blog(comfortwithtruth.substack.com) since 2011 and serving as a home church pastor since 2016. Cutchins and his lovely, fiery wife, Cheyenne, have five children and live in the North Georgia Mountains.

Printed in the United States
by Baker & Taylor Publisher Services